Aunt Daisy's Allotment

Written by James Clements
Illustrated by Richard Watson

Netty and Cora were visiting Aunt Daisy.

Aunt Daisy had hurt her foot.

Thank you for visiting me!

Netty

Cora

Are the **groups** of books **equal** or **unequal**? Are the **groups** of flowers **equal** or **unequal**? Are the **groups** of biscuits **equal** or **unequal**?

Aunt Daisy had an allotment where she kept chickens and grew different plants.

'I need some jobs doing on the allotment,' she said.

Netty and Cora looked at each other and smiled.

'We can do them!' said Netty.

Aunt Daisy was very glad. She wrote a list of all the jobs that needed to be done.

At the allotment ...

'It will take a long time to do all the jobs on the list,' said Netty. 'If only there was a way to speed things up!'

'We could build a machine to help us,' said Cora.

'Great idea!' replied Netty.

Are the **groups** of cabbages **equal** or **unequal**?

The monsters got to work building a machine. Luckily, there were lots of spare parts in Aunt Daisy's shed.

Soon the machine was ready.

'This machine will finish Aunt Daisy's jobs in no time!' said Netty.

The machine has four wheels. Are the wheels in **equal groups** or **unequal groups**?

The first job on the list was to let the chickens out.

Cora tapped some buttons on the machine. The machine rolled over to the chicken run and opened the door. The chickens rushed out.

Netty and Cora were very pleased.

Netty tapped some more buttons on the machine. 'Now it can do all the other jobs,' she said.

The machine collected the chickens' eggs and brought them over to the monsters.

'I told the machine to put the same number of eggs in each box,' said Netty.

Are the eggs in **equal groups** or **unequal groups**? Has the machine done what Netty told it to do?

However, when Cora looked in the boxes, she could see something was wrong. 'The machine hasn't put the same number of eggs in each box,' she said.

'Don't worry,' replied Netty.

 **How many equal groups** of eggs are there? **How many** eggs are in each **group**? There are two **groups** of four eggs.

The next job was to plant Aunt Daisy's new flowers.

'I told the machine to put the same number of flowers in each pot,' said Netty.

How many equal groups of flowers are there? **How many** flowers are in each **group**?

However, the monsters got a surprise when the machine threw the flowers into the air!

Netty and Cora quickly caught them before they fell on the ground.

'I think we should plant the flowers ourselves,' said Netty.

The next job was to pull out the weeds from the vegetable patch.

The monsters hoped the machine would do the right thing this time.

However, the machine started to pull out the carrots instead of the weeds!

'Quick, stop it!' shouted Cora.

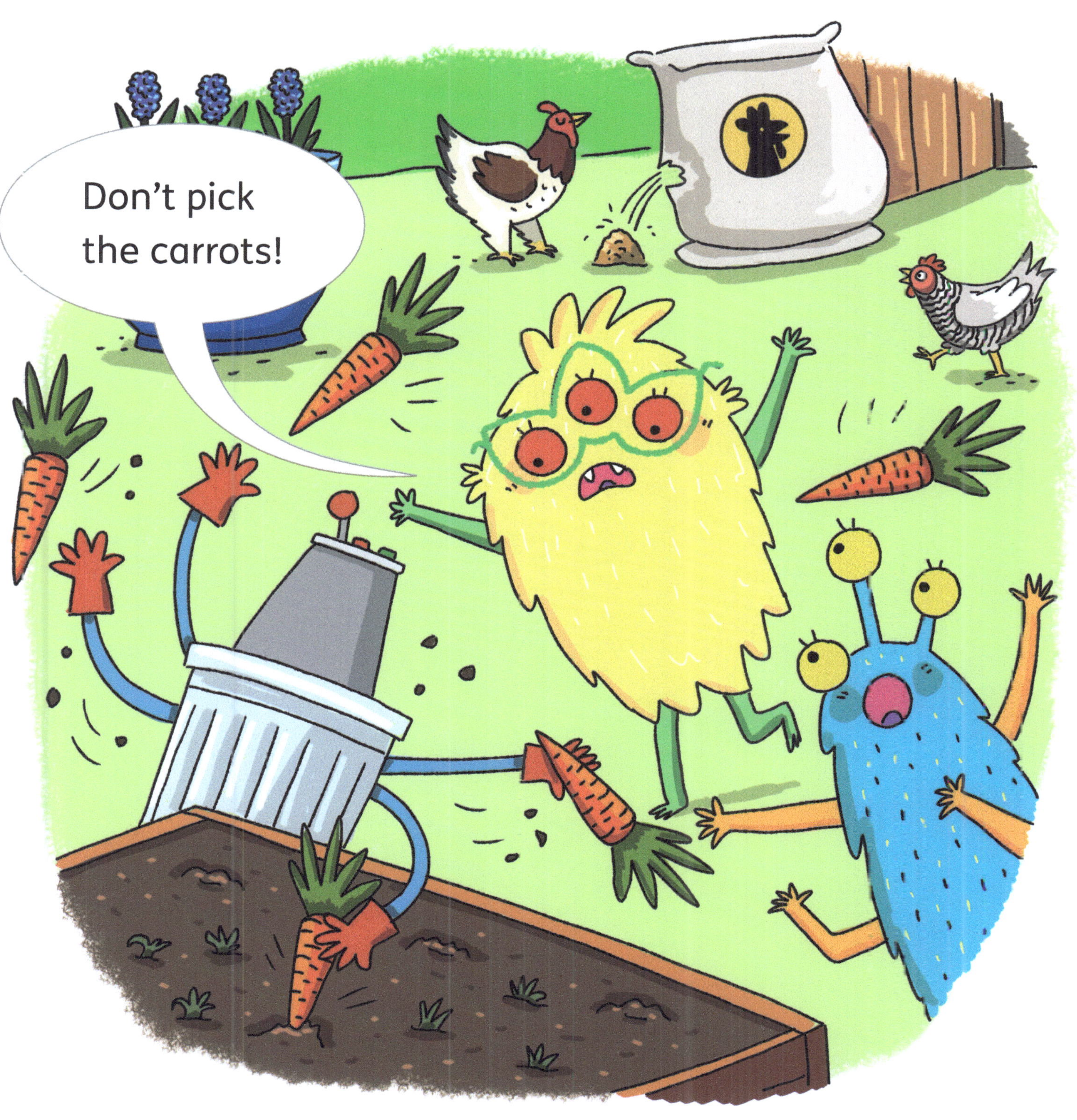

Netty ran to the machine and turned it off. With a loud clunk, the machine stopped.

'We will have to pull out the weeds ourselves,' said Cora.

Netty and Cora pulled out the weeds from the vegetable patch. Then they took the machine apart.

The carrots are in **unequal groups**. How could you make the **groups equal**?

Suddenly, Netty spotted the chickens eating a big pile of corn. 'Naughty chickens!' she cried.

The monsters tried to round up the chickens.

Netty and Cora put all the chickens back in their run and shut the door.

Finally, the monsters had finished all the jobs on Aunt Daisy's list. They collected the carrots and the eggs.

Netty and Cora went back to Aunt Daisy's house and knocked on the door. Aunt Daisy opened it with a big, beaming smile. Her foot was much better.

How many equal groups of carrots are there? **How many** carrots are in each **group**?

The monsters told Aunt Daisy about their machine.

'We're sorry, Aunt Daisy. The machine picked your carrots instead of the weeds,' explained Netty.

'Don't worry,' Aunt Daisy replied. 'The carrots were ready to be picked anyway!'

Aunt Daisy took the carrots into the kitchen and began chopping them up to make some soup.

Suddenly, she stopped. 'Oh, no,' she said. 'There was one job I forgot to put on the list. I forgot to ask you to feed the chickens!'

Look at the cakes on the plate. **How many equal groups** of berries are there? **How many** berries are in each **group**?

Netty and Cora grinned at each other.

'Don't worry, Aunt Daisy,' said Cora, giggling. 'The chickens had plenty of food.'

Aunt Daisy smiled with relief.

Help Aunt Daisy

Aunt Daisy wants to put the same amount of food on each plate.

Are the items in **equal groups** or **unequal groups**? If the **groups** are **unequal**, what do you need to do to make them **equal**?